*Spiritualism
and Theosophy*

By
Henry S. Olcott

Copyright © 2023 Lamp of Trismegistus. All rights reserved. No part of this publication may be reproduced or transmitted in any form or by any means, electronic or mechanical, including photocopying, recording, or by any information storage and retrieval system, without permission in writing from Lamp of Trismegistus. Reviewers may quote brief passages.

ISBN: 978-1-63118-629-5

*Esoteric Classics*

## Other Books in this Series and Related Titles

*Hypnotism and Mesmerism* by Annie Besant (978–1–63118–587–8)

*The Hidden Language of Symbolism* by Annie Besant (978–1–63118–585–4)

*Memory and Consciousness* by Besant & Blavatsky (978–1–63118–582–3)

*Occultism, Semi-Occultism & Pseudo Occultism* by A Besant (978–1–63118–577–9)

*Spiritual Life for Man* by Annie Besant (978–1–63118–573–1)

*The Mysteries* by Annie Besant (978–1–63118–572–4)

*Communication Between Different Worlds* by Annie Besant (978–1–63118–569–4)

*The Brotherhood of Religions* by Annie Besant (978–1–63118–563–2)

*Clairvoyance and Psychic Abilities* by A Besant &c (978-1-63118-403-1)

*Spiritual Progress and Practical Occultism* by H P Blavatsky (978–1–63118–583–0)

*Alchemy in the Nineteenth Century* by Helena P. Blavatsky (978-1-63118-446-8)

*Rosicrucians and Speculative Masonry in the Seventeenth Century* (978-1-63118-489-5)

*Qabbalistic Teachings and the Tree of Life* by M P Hall (978-1-63118-482-6)

*Early Masonic Symbolism* by Manly P Hall (978–1–63118–606–6)

*Fortune-Telling with Dice* by Astra Cielo (978-1-63118-466-6)

*History, Analysis and Secret Tradition of the Tarot* by Hall &c (978-1-63118-445-1)

*Crystal Vision Through Crystal Gazing* by Frater Achad (978-1-63118-455-0)

*Arcane Formulas or Mental Alchemy* by W W Atkinson (978-1-63118-459-8)

*The Machinery of the Mind* by Dion Fortune (978-1-63118-451-2)

*The A E Waite Reader: A Selection of Occult Essays* (978-1-63118-515-1)

*The Leadbeater Reader: A Selection of Occult Essays* (978-1-63118-483-3)

**Audio versions are also available on Audible, Amazon and Apple**

## Other Books in this Series and Related Titles

*Duties of a Theosophist* by Annie Besant (978-1-63118-628-8)

*The Book of the Nephilim* by Enoch (978-1-63118-627-1)

*Building Occult Character* by Besant & Leadbeater (978-1-63118-626-4)

*Ancient Egyptian Mysteries and Hieroglyphics, Modern Freemasonry & Initiation of the Pyramid* (978-1-63118-625-7) HC

*The Lost Book of Noah* by Noah (978-1-63118-624-0)

*The Acts of Saint Andrew* by Andrew (978-1-63118-623-3)

*The Acts of the Apostle John* by John (978–1–63118–622–6)

*Karmic Visions* by Helena P. Blavatsky (978–1–63118–621–9)

*The Ascension of Isaiah* by Isaiah (978-1-63118-620-2)

*The Mysteries of Mithra* by G R S Mead (978-1-63118-619-6)

*Second Book of Enoch* by Enoch (978-1-63118-617-2)

*Lost Keys of Freemasonry* by Manly P Hall (978-1-63118-616-5)

*Book of the Watchers* by Enoch (978-1-63118-615-8)

*Sepher Yetzirah and the Qabalah* by Manly P Hall (978-1-63118-614-1)

*Philosophy of Self-Knowledge* by Franz Hartmann (978-1-63118-613-4)

*Occult Symbolism of the Sun and Moon, the Goddess Isis and thee Solar Deities* by Manly P Hall (978–1–63118–611–0)

*Practical Theosophy* by Annie Besant (978–1–63118–610–3)

*The Human Body in Symbolism* by Manly P Hall (978–1–63118–609–7)

*Theosophical Basics* by William Q Judge (978–1–63118–608–0)

*The Hebrew Talisman* by Richard Harte (978–1–63118–607–3)

**Audio versions are also available on Audible, Amazon and Apple**

# Table of Contents

Introduction...7

Short Essay on Henry S. Olcott...9

*Spiritualism and Theosophy*...13

# INTRODUCTION

The word "esoteric" can be difficult to define. Esotericism in general can be seen less as a system of beliefs and more as a category, which encompasses numerous, different systems of beliefs. It's a bit of juxtaposition, since the word "esoteric" indicates something that few people know about, while the term itself broadly covers numerous philosophies, practices, areas of study and belief systems.

In a greater sense, Esotericism acts as a storehouse for secret knowledge, which is often considered ancient (by *tradition, if not by fact*), passed down from generation to generation, in private. At various times in history, simply possessing the knowledge of some of these subjects, was considered illegal and a jailable offence, if discovered. This usually included such general topics as Alchemy, Pharmacology, Qabalah, Hermeticism, Occultism, Ceremonial Magic, Astrology, Divination, Rosicrucianism and so on. Collectively, these areas of study were often referred to as the esoteric sciences.

Sometimes, the outer garment of a subject isn't esoteric, while what is hidden beneath it, is. As an example, Freemasonry isn't necessarily esoteric by nature (at *least not anymore)*, but certain signs, passwords and handshakes given to the candidate during their initiation, are in fact, esoteric, in the sense that they are hidden from the general public.

Today, in the twenty-first century, such topics are readily available at bookstores across the country, and numerous main-steam publishers offer beginners guides and coffee-table volumes on many of these subjects, intended for mass appeal. Books like *"The Secret"* have turned previously arcane topics into household knowledge. All that being the case, however, it isn't to say that there still aren't buried secrets to uncover, ancient wisdom being ignored and forgotten mysteries to be explored. In fact, it is often that we are only able to further our own studies by standing on the shoulders of these disappearing giants.

Lamp of Trismegistus is doing its part to help preserve humanity's esoteric history by making some of these classics available to those students who are seeking to unearth the knowledge of these ancient colossi.

So, be sure to check other titles from our *Esoteric Classics* series, as well as our *Occult Fiction, Theosophical Classics, Foundations of Freemasonry Series, Supernatural Fiction, Paranormal Research Series, Studies in Buddhism* and our *Christian Apocrypha Series*. You can also download the audio versions of most of these titles from Amazon, Apple or Audible, for learning on the go.

# A SHORT ESSAY ON HENRY S. OLCOTT

Henry Steel Olcott, a prominent figure in the late 19th century, was a multifaceted personality who gained renown as a lawyer, soldier, journalist, and investigator of spiritual phenomena. However, it was his exploration and contributions to Theosophy, the occult, and esoteric knowledge that distinguished him as a key figure in the spiritual movements of his era.

Born on August 2, 1832, in Orange, New Jersey, Olcott demonstrated a penchant for intellectual pursuits from an early age. Despite a varied and impressive career that included service in the American Civil War and the United States Department of Agriculture, it was his intersection with spiritualism and theosophy that would define his legacy.

The turning point in Olcott's spiritual journey was his exposure to the spiritualist movement of the late 19th century. Intrigued by the assertions of spirit communication, he delved into the movement, examining mediums and their alleged supernatural abilities. His collaboration with Helena Petrovna Blavatsky, a famous occultist, in 1874, ushered him into the realm of Theosophy.

Theosophy, a philosophical and religious movement emphasizing spiritual wisdom, appealed to Olcott due to its emphasis on a universal brotherhood, irrespective of religion, race, and gender, and its promotion of the study of comparative religion, philosophy, and science. He saw in Theosophy an opportunity to reconcile the scientific and spiritual aspects of existence.

Together with Blavatsky, Olcott co-founded the Theosophical Society in 1875. As its first president, he had an instrumental role in shaping the Society's doctrines and direction. Despite facing initial criticisms and skepticism, Olcott remained undeterred in his pursuit of esoteric knowledge and committed to spreading Theosophy's principles.

Olcott's involvement in Theosophy and the occult was characterized by an open-minded approach and an unyielding desire to explore the boundaries of human understanding. He was a firm advocate of spiritual development and was fascinated by Eastern religions, particularly Buddhism and Hinduism. In his view, these ancient wisdom traditions offered invaluable insights into human nature and the universe, which he believed were harmonious with Theosophical principles.

In 1880, Olcott and Blavatsky moved to India, a decision that significantly influenced the direction of the Theosophical Society and heightened its interest in Eastern spiritual traditions. Olcott's fascination with Buddhism led him to become an ardent supporter of the Buddhist revival in Sri Lanka. His contributions to the Buddhist education system and his efforts to reconcile differences among Buddhist sects were highly appreciated.

Olcott's interest in esotericism extended beyond Theosophy and Buddhism. He actively sought to bridge the gap between science and religion, believing that the two could coexist harmoniously. His work, "The Buddhist Catechism", articulates this viewpoint, asserting that Buddhism and science are inherently complementary.

Moreover, Olcott's curiosity was piqued by the mysticism within Hinduism, and he devoted considerable time to studying Hindu scriptures and understanding the underlying philosophy. This exploration of Hinduism broadened the horizons of Theosophy, making it more inclusive and appealing to a wider audience.

Olcott's commitment to Theosophy and his explorations into the occult were far from a mere fascination; they constituted a spiritual mission that he pursued with devotion and dedication. He was instrumental in broadening the appeal of the Theosophical Society and laying the groundwork for the society's enduring influence on global spirituality and metaphysical thought.

Henry Steel Olcott died on February 17, 1907, but his contributions to Theosophy and the esoteric continue to resonate in contemporary spiritual and philosophical discourse.

Even after Olcott's death, his influence on esoteric thought remains significant. He left behind a rich legacy of writings, lectures, and other works that continue to inspire and enlighten those interested in spiritual wisdom and the study of the occult. His vision of a unified spiritual understanding, transcending narrow religious confines, and embracing a more comprehensive and inclusive perspective of reality, endures within the Theosophical Society and similar organizations worldwide.

Further, Olcott's dedication to interfaith understanding, particularly between Eastern and Western religions, has had a lasting impact. His work in bridging cultural and religious gaps has been instrumental in fostering dialogue and mutual respect among diverse religious traditions. The empathy and respect he showed towards the spiritual traditions of the East, especially Buddhism and Hinduism, was path-breaking for its time, sparking greater interest in Eastern philosophy in the West.

Beyond theosophy and occult studies, Olcott's commitment to educational reforms, particularly in Sri Lanka, has had a profound and long-lasting impact. His efforts led to the establishment of several Buddhist schools in the country, contributing significantly to the propagation and preservation of Buddhism in the region.

In conclusion, Henry Steel Olcott, as a pioneering figure in the exploration of Theosophy, the occult, and the esoteric, has left an indelible mark on spiritual and philosophical thought. His open-minded approach to spiritualism, keen interest in bridging the East and the West, and dedication to expanding human understanding's boundaries remain inspirational. The vibrancy and diversity of his work continue to stimulate theosophical and esoteric studies, ensuring that his legacy endures long beyond his lifetime.

# SPIRITUALISM AND THEOSOPHY

THIRTEEN years ago, one of the most eminent of modern American jurists, John W. Edmonds, Chief Justice of the Supreme Court of New York, declared in a London magazine that there were then at least ten millions of Spiritualists in the Unites States of America. No man was so well qualified at that time as he, to express an opinion upon this subject, for not only was he in correspondence with persons in all parts of the country, but the noble virtue of the man as well as his learning, his judicial impartiality and conservatism, made him a most competent and convincing witness. And another authority, a publicist of equally unblemished private and public reputation, the Hon. Robert Dale Owen, while endorsing Judge Edmonds' estimate adds [*The Debatable Land between This World and the Next,* p 174- London Ed. 1874] that there are at least an equal number in the rest of Christendom. To avoid all chance of exaggeration he, however, deducts one-fourth from both amounts and (in 1874) writes the sum-total of the so-called Spiritualists at fifteen millions. But whatever the aggregate of believers in the alleged present open intercourse between our worlds of substance and shadow, it is a known fact that the number embraces some of the most acute intellects of the day. It is no question now of the self- deceptions of boors and hysterical chambermaids with which we have to deal. Those who would deny the reality of these contemporaneous phenomena, must confront a multitude of our most capable men of science who have exhausted the resources of their profession to determine the nature of the force at work, and been baffled in seeking any other explanation than the one of trans-sepulchral agency of some kind or other. Beginning with Robert Hare, the inventor of the oxy-hydrogen blow-pipe and Nestor of American Chemistry, and ending with Fr. Zollner, Professor of Physical Astronomy in Leipzig University, the list of these converted experimentalists includes a succession of adepts of Physical Science of the highest professional rank. Each of them except perhaps Zollner, who wished to verify his theory of a fourth dimension of space - began the task of investigation with the avowed purpose of exposing the alleged fraud, in the interests of public morals; and each was transformed into an avowed believer in the reality of mediumistic phenomena by the irresistible logic of facts.

The apparatuses devised by these men of science to test the mediumistic power have been in the highest degree ingenious. They have been of four different kinds: (a) machines to determine whether electrical or magnetic currents were operating; (b) whether the movement of heavy articles, such as tables touched by the medium, was caused by either conscious or unconscious muscular contraction; (c) whether intelligent communications may be received by a sitter under circumstances precluding any possible trickery by the medium; and (d) what are the conditions for the manifestation of this new form of energy and the extreme limitations of its action. Of course, in an hour's lecture, I could not describe a tenth part of these machines, but I may take two as illustrating two of the above-enumerated branches of research. The first is to be found described in Professor Hare's work. The medium and enquirer sit facing each other, the medium's hands resting upon a bit of board so hung and adjusted that, whether he presses on the board or not, he merely moves that and nothing else. In front of the visitor is a dial, like a clock face, around which are arranged the letters of the alphabet, the ten numerals, the words "Yes," "No," "Doubtful," and perhaps others. A pointer, or hand, that is connected with a lever, the other end of which is so placed as to receive any current flowing through the medium's system, but not to be affected by any mechanical pressure he may exert upon the hand-rest, travels around the dial and indicates the letters or words the communicating intelligence wishes noted down. The back of the dial being towards the medium, he, of course, cannot see what the pointer is doing, and if the enquirer conceals from him the paper on which he is noting down the communication, he cannot have even a suspicion of what is being said.

The other contrivance is described and illustrated in the monograph entitled *Researches in the Phenomena of Spiritualism*, by Mr William Crookes, F.R.S., Editor of the *Quarterly Journal of Science*, and one of the most successful experimental chemists of our day. A mahogany board, 36 inches long by 9 1/2 inches wide, and 1 inch thick, rests at one end upon a table, upon a strip cut to a knife edge; at the other end it is suspended by a spring-balance, fitted with an automatic registering apparatus, and hung from a firm tripod. On the table end of the board, and directly over the fulcrum, is placed a large vessel filled with water. In this water dips, to the depth of 1 1/2 inches from the surface, a copper vessel, with bottom perforated so as to let the water enter it; which copper vessel is supported by a fixed iron ring, attached to an iron stand that rests on the floor. The medium is to dip his hands in the water in the copper vessel, and as this is solidly supported by its own stand and ring, and nowhere touches the glass vessel holding the water, you see that, should there occur any depression of the pointer on the spring-balance at the extreme end of the board, it unmistakably indicates that a current of force, weighable in foot pounds, is passing through the medium's body. Well, both Dr Hare, with his apparatus, and Mr Crookes, with his, obtained the desired proof that certain phenomena of mediumship do occur without the interference, either honest or dishonest, of the medium. To the power thus manifested, Mr Crookes, upon the suggestion of the late Mr Serjeant Cox, gave the appropriate name of Psychic Force, and as such it will hereafter be designated by me in this lecture.

I mention these two mechanical contrivances merely to show those who, perhaps, have never enquired into the matter, but have nevertheless fallen into the common error of thinking the phenomena to be all deceptions, that the utmost care has been taken by the cleverest scientists to guard against the possibility of fraud in the course of their experiments. If ever there was a fact of science proved, it is that a new and most mysterious force of *some* kind has been manifesting itself since March, 1848, when this mighty modern epiphany was ushered in, with a shower of raps, at an obscure hamlet in New York State. Beginning with these percussive sounds, it has since displayed its energy in a hundred different phenomena, each inexplicable upon any known hypothesis of science, and in almost if not quite, every country of our globe. To advocate its study, expound its laws, and disseminate its intelligent manifestations, hundreds of journals and books have from time to time been published in different languages; the movement has its schools and churches, or meeting halls, its preachers and teachers; and a body of men and women, numbering thousands at the least, are devoting their whole time and vital strength to the profession of mediumship. These sensitives, or "psychics," are to be found in every walk of life, in the palaces of royalty as well as the labourer's cottage, and their psychical, or mediumistic, gifts are as various as their individualities.

What has caused this world-wide expansion of the new movement, and reconciled the public to such a vast sacrifice of comfort, time, money, and social consequence? What has spurred on so many of the most intelligent people in all lands, of all sects and races, to continue investigating? What has kept the faith alive in so many millions, despite a multitude of sickening exposures of the rascality of mediums, of the demoralizing tendency of ill-regulated mediumship, and the average puerility and frequent mendaciousness of the communications received? This: that a hope has sprung up in the human breast that at last man may have experimental proof of his survival after bodily death and a glimpse, if not a full revelation, and his future destiny. All these millions cling, like the drowning man to his bank, to the one hope that the old, old questions of the What? the Whence? the Whither? will now be solved, once and for all time. Glance through the literature of Spiritualism and you shall see what joy, what consolation, and what perfect rest and courage these weird, often exasperating, phenomena of the séance room have imparted. Tears have ceased to flow from a myriad eyes when the dead are laid away out of sight, and broken ties of love and friendship are no longer regarded by these believers as snapped for ever. The tempest no longer affrights as it did, and the terrors of battle and pestilence have lost their greatest power for the modern Spiritualist. The supposed intercourse with the dead and their messages have sapped the infallible authority of dogmatic theology. The Spiritualist with the eye of his new faith now sees the dim outlines of a Summer Land where we live and are occupied much as upon Earth. The tomb, instead of seeming the mouth of a void darkness, has come to look merely like a somber gateway to a country of sunlight brightness and never-ending progression towards the crowning state of perfectibility. Nay, so definite have become the fancy pictures of this Summer Land, that one constantly reads of baby children growing in spirit life to be adults; of colleges and academies for mortal guidance, presided over by the world's departed sages; and even of nuptial unions between living men or women and the denizens of the spirit world! A case in point is that of the Rev. Thomas Lake Harris - founder of the socialistic community on Lake Erie, which Laurence Oliphant and his mother have joined - who gives out that he is duly married to a female spirit and that a child has blessed their union! Another case is that of the marriage of two spirits in the presence of mortal witnesses, by a living clergyman, which was reported last year in the Spiritualistic papers - a Mr Pierce, son of an ex-President of the United States and long since dead, is said to have "materialized," that is, made for himself a visible, tangible body, at the house of a certain American medium, and been married by a minister summoned for the occasion, to a lady spirit who died at the very tender age of seven months and who, now grown into a blooming lass, was also materialized for the ceremony! The vows exchanged and the blessings given, the happy couple sat at table with invited friends, and, after drinking a toast or two, vanished -- dress-coat, white gloves, satin, lace and all - into thin air! This you will call the tomfoolery of Spiritualism, and you will be right; but, nevertheless, it serves to show

how clear and definite, not to say brutally materialistic, are the views of the other world order which have replaced the old, vague dread that weighed us down with gloomy doubts. Up to a certain point this state of mind is a decided gain, but I am sorry to say Spiritualists have passed that, and become dogmatists. Little by little a body of enthusiasts is forming, who would throw a halo of sanctity around the medium, and, by doing away with test conditions, invite to the perpetration of gross frauds. Mediums actually caught red-handed in trickery, with their paraphernalia of traps, false panels, wigs and puppets about them, have been able to make their dupes regard them as martyrs to the rage of sceptics, and the damning proofs of their guilt, as having been secretly supplied by the unbelievers themselves to strike a blow at their holy cause! The voracious credulity of a large body of Spiritualists has begotten nine-tenths of the dishonest tricks of mediums. As Mr Crookes truly observed - in his preliminary article in the *Quarterly Journal of Science*: "In the countless number of recorded observations I have read, there appear to be few instances of meetings held for the express purpose of getting the phenomena under test conditions." Still, though this is true, it is also most certain that within the past thirty-two years, enquirers into the phenomena have been vouchsafed thousands upon thousands of proofs that they occur under conditions quite independent of the physical agency of persons present, and that intelligence, sometimes of a striking character, is displayed in the control of the occult force or forces producing the phenomena. It is this great reserve of test fact upon which rests, like a rock upon its base, the invincible faith of the millions of Spiritualists. This body of individual experiences is the rampart behind which they entrench themselves whenever the outside world of sceptics looks to see the whole "delusion crumble under the assault of some new *buna* critic, or the shame of the latest exposure of false mediumship or tricking mediums. It ought by this time to have been discovered that it is worse than useless to try to ridicule away the actual evidence of one's senses; or to make a man who has seen a heavy weight self-lifted and suspended in air, or writing done without contact, or a human form melt before his eyes, believe any theory that all mediumistic phenomena are due to "muscular contractions," "expectant attention," or "unconscious cerebration". It is because of their attempts to do this, that men of science, as a body, are regarded with such compassionate scorn by the experienced psychologist. Mr Wallace tells us that, after making careful inquiry, he has never found one man who, after having acquired a good personal knowledge of the chief phases of the phenomena, has afterwards come to disbelieve in their reality. And this is my own experience also. Some have ceased to be "Spiritualists" and turned Catholics, but they have never doubted the phenomena being real. It will be a happy day, one to be hailed with joy by every lover of true science, when our modern professors shall rid themselves of the conceited idea that knowledge was born in our days, and question in an humble spirit the records of archaic science.

We have seen that the existence of a force-current has been proved by the experiments of Dr Hare and Mr Crookes, so we need trouble ourselves no more with the many crude conjectures about table-moving, chair-lifting, and the raps being the result of the muscular energy of the medium or the visitor, but pass on to notice some of the forms in which this force has displayed its dynamic energies. These may be separated into phenomena indicating intelligence and conveying information, and purely physical manifestations of energy. Of the first class, the one demanding first place is the so-called "spirit-rap". By these simple signals the whole modern movement called Spiritualism was ushered in. These audible concussions vary in degree from the sound of a pinhead ticking to that of blows by a hammer or bludgeon powerful enough to shatter a mahogany table. The current of psychic force producing them seems to depend upon the state of the medium's system, in combination with the electric and hygrometric condition of the atmosphere. With either unpropitious, the raps, if heard at all, are faint; with both in harmony, they are loudest and most persistent. Of themselves these rapping phenomena are sufficiently wonderful, but they become a hundredfold more so when we find that through them communications can be obtained from intelligences claiming to be our dead friends: communications which often disclose secrets known only to the enquirer and no other person present; and even, in rare cases, giving out facts which no one then in the room was aware of, and which had to be verified later by consulting old records or distant witnesses. A more beautiful form of the rap is the sound of music, as of a stroke on a cut glass vessel, or a silver bell, heard either under the medium's hand or in the air. Such a phenomenon has been often noticed by the Rev Stainton Moses, "M. A. Oxon.," in his own house, and Mr Alfred R Wallace describes it as occurring in the presence of Miss Nichol, now Mrs Volckmann, at Mr Wallace's own house. An empty wine-glass was put upon a table and held by Miss Nichol and a Mr Humphrey to prevent any vibration. Mr Wallace tells us that, "after a short interval of silence an exquisitely delicate sound, as of tapping a glass, was heard, which increased to clear silvery notes like the tinkling of a glass bell. These continued in varying degrees for some minutes, etc." Again, Mr Wallace, says that when a German lady sang some of her national songs "most delicate music, like a fairy musical box, accompanied her throughout . . . This was in the dark, but hands were joined all the time." Several of the persons in this present audience have been permitted by Madame Blavatsky to hear these dulcet fairy-bells tinkle since she came to Simla. But they have heard them in full light, without any joining of hands, and in whatsoever place she chose to order them. The phenomenon is the same as that of Miss Nichol, but the conditions very different; and of that I will have something to say further on.

Mr Crookes found the force-current to be extremely variable in the same medium on different days, and, in the medium from minute to minute, its flow was highly erratic. In his book he gives a number of cuts to illustrate these variations, as well as of the ingenious apparatus he employed to detect them.

Among many thousands of communications from the alleged spirits that have been given to the public, and which for most part contain only trivial messages about family or other personal affairs, the details of which were at least known to the enquirers to whom addressed, and which might be attributed to thought-reading, we occasionally come across some that require some other explanation.

I refer to those the details mentioned in which are unknown to anyone present at the sitting. Mr Stainton Moses records one such - a case in which a message was given in London, purporting to come from an old man who had been a soldier in America in the war of 1812 and to have died there. None in London had ever heard of such a person, but upon causing a search to be made in the records of the American War Department, at Washington, the man's name was found and full corroborative proofs of the London message were obtained. Not having access to books here, I am obliged to quote from memory, but I think you will find my facts essentially correct. In another case, for which Mr J. M. Peebles vouches, that gentleman received, either in America or somewhere else, far away from England, a message from an alleged spirit who said he lived and died at York, and that if Mr Peebles would search the records of that ancient city the spirit's statements would be found strictly true. In process of time he did visit York and search old birth and burial registers, and there, sure enough, he found just the data he had been promised.

Besides communicating by raps, the alleged spirits have employed many other devices to impart intelligence to the living. Such, among others, are the independent writing of messages upon paper laid on the floor under a table or in a closed drawer, between the leaves of a closed book, or on the ceiling or walls, or one's linen; in none of these cases there being any human hand near by when the writing has been done. All these phenomena I have seen occur in full light and under circumstances where trickery or deception was impossible. I have also had satisfactory experience of the rare mediumistic powers of Dr

Henry Slade, who, you recollect, was arrested on a trumped-up charge of dishonesty in London, but afterwards gave Zollner and his brother *savants* of Leipzig, Aksakof, Boutlerof and Wagner, of St Petersburg, and the Grand Duke Constantine, a series of most complete tests. It was Madame Blavatsky and I who sent Dr Slade from America to Europe in 1876. A very high personage having ordered a scientific investigation of Spiritualism, the professors of the Imperial University of St Petersburg organized an experimental Committee, and we two were specially requested by this Committee to select, out of the best American mediums, one whom we could recommend for the test. After much investigation we chose Dr Slade, and the necessary funds for his expenses having been remitted to me, he was in due time sent abroad. Before I would recommend him I exacted the condition that he should place himself in the hands of a Committee of the Theosophical Society for testing. I purposely selected as members of that Committee men who were either pronounced sceptics or quite unacquainted with Spiritualistic phenomena. Slade was tested thoroughly for several weeks, and when the Committee's Report was finally made, the following facts were certified to as having occurred. Messages were written inside double slates, sometimes tied and sealed together, while they either lay upon the table in full view of all, or were laid upon the heads of members of the Committee, or held flat against the under surface of the table-top, or held in a Committee man's hand without the medium touching it. We also saw detached hands - that is, hands that floated or darted through the air and had no arm or body attached to them. These hands would clutch at our watch chains, grasp our limbs, touch our hands, take the slates or other objects from us under the table, remove our handkerchiefs from our coat-pockets, etc. And all this, mind you, in the light, where every movement of the medium could be as plainly seen as any that my present hearers might make now.

Another form of signaling is the compulsory writing of messages by a medium whose arm and hand are controlled against his volition by some invisible power. Not only thousands, but lakhs of pages have been written in this way, some of the subject-matter being worth keeping, but the greater part trash.Another method is the impression by the unseen intelligence upon the sensitive brain of a medium, of ideas and words outside his own knowledge, such as foreign languages, names of deceased persons, the circumstances of their deaths, requests as to the disposal of property, directions for the recovery of lost documents or valuables, information about murders or about distant tragedies of which they were the victims, diagnoses of hidden diseases and suggestions for remedies, etc. You will find many examples of each of these groups of phenomena on record and well attested.

A very interesting anecdote is related in Mr Dale Owen's *Debatable Land*, about the identification of an old spinet that was purchased at a Paris bric-a-brac shop by the grandson of the famous composer, Bach. The details are very curious and you will do well to read them, lack of time preventing my entering more at length into the subject now.

But of all the forms of intelligent communication from the other world to ours, of course none is to be compared for startling realism with that of the audible voice. I have heard these voices of every volume, from the faintest whisper close to the ear, sounding like the sigh of a zephyr through the trees, to the stentorian roar that would almost shake the room and might almost have been heard rods away from the house. I have heard them speak to me through paper tubes, through metal trumpets, and through empty space. And in the case of the world-famous medium, William Eddy, the voices spoke in four languages of which the medium knew not a word. Of the Eddy phenomena, I will speak anon.

One of the prettiest - I would say the most charming of all, but for the recollection of the fairy-like music of mediumistic phenomena - is the bringing of fresh, dew-be gemmed flowers, plants and vines, and of living creatures such as birds, gold-fish and butterflies into closed rooms, while the medium was in no state to bring them herself. I have myself, in friends' houses, held the hands of a medium whom I had first put into a bag that was fastened about her neck with a sealed draw-string, and with no confederate in the house, have had the whole table covered with flowers and plants, and birds come fluttering into my lap from goodness knows where. And this with every door and window fastened, and sealed with strips of paper so that no one could enter from the outside. These phenomena happened mostly in the dark, but once I saw a tree-branch brought in the daylight. I was present once at a séance in America when a gentleman asked that the "spirits might bring him a heather-plant from the Scottish moors, and suddenly, one pulled up by the roots and with the fresh soil clinging to them, was dropped on the table directly in front of him.

A highly interesting example of the non-intelligent class of phenomena came under my notice in the course of our search after a medium to send to Russia. A lady medium, named Mrs Youngs, had a reputation for causing a pianoforte to rise from the floor and sway in time to her playing upon the instrument. Madame Blavatsky and I went one evening to see her, and what happened was reported in the New York papers of the following day. As she sat at the piano playing, it certainly did tilt on the two outer legs - those farthest from her - and, with the other two, raised six or eight inches from the ground, move in time to the music. Mrs Youngs then went to one end of the piano and, laying a single finger against the under side of the case, lifted the tremendous weight with the greatest ease. If any of you care to compute the volume of psychic force exerted, try to lift one end of a 7 1/2 octave piano six inches from the floor. To test the reality of this phenomenon I had brought with me a raw egg, which I held in the palm of my hand, and pressed it lightly against the under side of the piano case at one end. I then caused the medium to lay the palm of her hands against the back of mine that held the egg, and told her to command the piano to rise. A moment's pause only ensued when, to my surprise, one end of the piano did rise without so much pressure upon the egg as to break the shell. I think that this, as a test of the actuality of a psychic force, was almost as conclusive an experiment as the water-basin and spring- balance of Mr Crookes. At least it was to myself, for I can affirm that the medium did not press as much as an ounce weight against the back of my hand, and it is quite certain that but very few ounces of pressure would have broken the thin shell of the egg.

One of the most undeniable manifestations of independent force is the raising and moving of a heavy weight without human contact. This I, in common with many other investigators, have witnessed. Sitting at a table in the centre of my own lighted drawing-room, I have seen the piano raised and moved a foot away from the wall, and a heavy leather armchair run from a distant corner towards, and touch us, when no one was within a dozen feet of either of them. On another occasion my late friend and chemical teacher, Professor Mapes, who was a very corpulent person, and two other men, equally stout, were requested to seat themselves on a mahogany dining table, and all were raised from the ground, the medium merely laying one hand on the top of the table. At Mrs Youngs' house, on the evening before noticed, as many persons as could sit on the top of the piano were raised with the instrument while she was playing a waltz. The records are full of instances where rooms, or even whole houses were caused by the occult force to shake and tremble as though a hurricane were blowing, though the air was quite still.

And you have the testimony of Lords Lindsay, Aberdare, Dunraven, and other unimpeachable witnesses, to the fact of a medium's body having floated around the room and sailed out of a window, seventy feet from the ground and into another window. This was in an obscure light, but I have seen, in the twilight, a person raised out of her chair until her head was as high as the globes of the chandelier, and then gently lowered down again.

You see I am telling you stories so wonderful that it is impossible for anyone to fully credit them without the corroboration of his own personal experience. Believe me, I would not tell them at all - for no man desires to have his word doubted - unless I knew perfectly well that such phenomena have been seen hundreds of times in nearly every land under the sun, and can be seen by anyone who will give time to the investigation. Despite my disclaimer, you may think that I am taking it for granted that you are quite as well satisfied as myself of the reality of the mediumistic phenomena, but I assure you I am not. I am always keeping in mind that, no matter what respect an auditor may have for my integrity and cleverness, no matter how plainly he may see that I have no ulterior motive to deceive him - yet he *cannot* believe without himself having had the same demonstrative evidences that I have had. He will - because he must - reflect that such things as these are outside the usual experience of men, and that, as Hume puts it, it is more reasonable to believe any man a liar than that the even course of natural law should be disturbed. True, that assumes the absurd premise that the average man knows what are the limitations of natural law, but we never consider our own opinions absurd, no matter how others may regard them. So, knowing, as I have just remarked, that what I describe has been seen by thousands, and may be seen by thousands more at any time, I proceed with my narrative as one who tells the truth and fears no impeachment. It is a great wonder what we are having shown us in our days, and apart from the solemn interest which attaches to the problem whether or not the dead are communing with us, the scientific importance of these facts cannot be undervalued. From the first - that is to say, throughout my twenty- eight years of observations - I have pursued my inquiry in this spirit, believing that it was of prime importance to mankind to ascertain all that could be learnt about man's powers and the forces of nature about him.

What I shall now relate about my adventures at the Eddy Homestead in Vermont, America, will tax your indulgence more than all that has preceded. For some years previous to 1874, I had taken an active interest in mediumistic phenomena. Nothing surpassingly novel had been reported as occurring, and the intelligence communicated through mediums was not usually instructive enough to induce one to leave his books and the company of their great authors. But in that year it was rumoured that at a remote village, in the valley of the Green Mountains, an illiterate farmer and his equally ignorant brother were being visited daily by the "materialized," souls of the departed, who could be seen, heard and, in cases, touched by any visitor. This tempting novelty I determined to witness, for it certainly transcended in interest and importance everything that had ever been heard of in any age. Accordingly, in August of that year, I went to Chittenden, the village in question, and, with a single brief intermission of ten days, remained there until the latter part of October. I hope you will believe that I adopted every possible precaution against being befooled by village trickery. The room of the ghosts was a large chamber occupying the whole upper floor of a two-story wing of the house. It was perhaps twenty feet wide by forty long - I speak from memory. Below were two rooms - a kitchen and a pantry; a kitchen chimney was in the gable end, of course, and passed through the séance room to the roof. It projected into the room two feet, and at the right, between it and the side of the house, was a plastered closet with a door next to the chimney. A window, two feet square, had been cut in the outer wall of the closet to admit air. Running across this end of the large room was a narrow platform, raised about 18 inches from the floor, with a step to mount by at the extreme left, and a handrail or baluster along the front edge of the platform. Every evening, after the last meal, William Eddy, a stout-built, square-shouldered, hard-handed farmer, would go upstairs, hang a thick, woollen shawl across the doorway, enter the closet and seat himself on a low chair that stood at the extreme end. The visitors, who sometimes numbered forty of an evening, were accommodated on benches placed within a few feet of the platform. Horatio Eddy sat on a chair in front, and discoursed doleful music on a fiddle and led the singing - if such it might be called without causing Mozart to turn in his grave; a feeble light was given by a kerosene lamp placed on the floor at the end of the room farthest from the platform, in an old drum from which both heads had been removed. Though the light was certainly very dim, yet it sufficed to enable us to see if anyone left his seat, and to distinguish through the gloom the height and costumes of the visitors from the other world. At a first sitting this was difficult, but practice soon accustomed one's eyes to the conditions.

After an interval of singing and fiddle-scraping, sometimes of five, sometimes of twenty or thirty minutes, we would see the shawl stirred, it would be pushed aside, and out upon the platform would step some figure. It might be a man, woman or child, a decrepit veteran or a babe carried in a woman's arms. The figure would have nothing at all of the supernatural or ghostly about it. A stranger entering at the other end of the room would simply fancy that a living mortal was standing there ready to address an audience. Its dress would be the one it wore in life, its face, hands, feet, gestures, perfectly natural. Sometimes, it would call the name of the living friend it had come to meet. If it were strong, the voice would be of the natural tone; if weak, the words came in faint whispers; if still more feeble, there was no voice at all, but the figure would stand leaning against the chimney or hand-rail while the audience asked in turn - "Is it for me?" and it either bowed its head or caused raps to sound on the wall when the right one asked the question. Then the anxious visitor would lean forward, and scan the figure's appearance in the dim light, and often we would hear the joyful cry "Oh! Mother, Father, Sister, Brother, Son, Daughter," or what not, "I know you". Then the weird visitor would be seen to bow, or stretch out its hands, and then, seeming to gather the last strength that remained to it in its evanescent frame, glide into the closet again, and drop the shawl before the hungry gaze of the eyes that watched it. But, sometimes, the form would last much longer. Several times I saw come out of the closet an aged lady clad in Quaker costume, with lawn cap and kerchief pinned across her bosom, grey dress and long, housewifely apron, and, calling her son to the platform, seat herself in a chair beside him, and, after kissing him fondly, talk for some minutes with him in low tones about family matters. All the while she would be absently folding the hem of her apron into tucks, and smoothing them out again, and so continuing the thing over and over, just as - her son told me - she was in the habit of doing while alive. More than once, just as she was ready to disappear, this gentleman would take her arm in his, come to the baluster, and say that he was requested by his old mother, whom we saw there, although she had been dead many years, to certify that it was, indeed, she herself and no deception, and bid them realize that man lives beyond the grave and so live here as to ensure their happiness then.

I will not attempt to give you, in these few minutes of our lecture, even the bare outline of my observations during those eventful weeks. Suffice it to say that I saw as many as seventeen of these *revenants* in a single evening, and that, from first to last, I saw about five hundred. There were a certain few figures that seemed especially attached to the medium's sphere of influence, but the rest were the appearances of friends of the strangers who daily flocked to the place from the most distant localities - some as far away as 2,000 miles. There were Americans and Europeans, Africans and Asiatics, Red Indians of our prairies and white people; each wearing his familiar dress and some even carrying their familiar weapons. One evening, the figure of a Kurd, a man whom Madame Blavatsky had known in Kurdistan, stepped from the closet, clad in his tall cap, high boots and picturesque clothes. In the shawl twisted about his waist were thrust a curved sword and other small arms. His hands were empty, but after salaaming my friend in his native fashion, lo! his right hand held a twelve foot spear which bore below the steel head a tuft of feathers. Now, supposing this farmer medium to have been ever so much a cheat, whence, in that secluded hamlet, did he procure this Kurdish dress, the belt, the arms and the spear at a moment's notice? - for Madame Blavatsky had but just arrived at Chittenden, and neither I nor anyone else knew who she was, nor whence she had come. All my experiences there were described by me, first in a series of letters to a New York journal, and afterwards in book form,* [*People from the Other World*] and I must refer the curious to that record for details, both as to what was seen and what precautions I took against deception. Two suspicions have doubtless occurred to your minds while I have been speaking - (a) that some confederate or confederates got access to the medium through the closet window, or dresses and dolls were passed up to him from below through a trap or sliding panel. Of course, that would occur to anyone with the least ingenuity of thought. It occurred to me, and this is what I did. I procured a ladder and on the outside of the house tacked a piece of mosquito net over the entire window, sash frame and all, sealing the tack-heads with wax, and stamping each with my signet ring. This effectively prevented any nonsense from that quarter. And then, calling to my help an architect and a clever Yankee inventor and mechanic, with those gentlemen I made a minute, practical examination of the chimney, the floor, the platform, the rooms below and the lumber-loft overhead. We were all perfectly satisfied that if there was any trickery in the case, it was done by William Eddy himself without confederacy, and that if he used theatrical dresses or properties, he must carry them in with him. In the little narrow hole of a closet there was neither a candle, mirror, brush, wig, clothes, water-basin, towel, cosmetic, nor any other of the actor's paraphernalia, nor, to speak the truth, had the poor farmer the money to buy them with. He took no fee for his séances, and visitors were charged only a very small sum for their board and lodging. I have sat smoking with him in his kitchen until it was time for the séance to begin, gone with him to the upper chamber, examined the closet before he entered it, searched his person, and then seen the selfsame wonderful figures come out as usual in their various dresses. I think I may claim to have proceeded cautiously, for Mr A. R. Wallace, F.R.S., quoted, and eulogized my book in his recent controversy with Professor W.B. Carpenter. Carpenter himself went to America to enquire into my character for veracity, and publicly admitted it to be unimpeachable. Professor Wagner, of St Petersburg, reviewed the work in a special pamphlet, in which he affirms that I fulfilled every requirement of scientific research, and three European psychological societies elected me Honorary Member. It should also be noted that four years of very responsible and intricate examinations, on behalf of the War Department - during our late American War, the proofs of which service have been shown by me to the Indian authorities - qualified me to conduct this inquiry with at least a tolerable certainty that I would not be imposed upon. Having then seen all that has now been outlined to you, will you wonder that I should have been thoroughly convinced of the reality of a large group of psychic phenomena, that science helplessly tried to offer some explanation for? And can you be surprised that whatever man of science has, since 1848, seriously and patiently investigated modern Spiritualism, he has become a convert, no matter what may have been his religious belief or professional bias?

The mention of religion leads me to a certain fact. While the Protestant Church has, in our time, ever resolutely denied the reality of such manifestations of occult agencies, the Church of Rome has always admitted them to be true. In her rubrics there are special forms of exorcism, and when Miss Laura Edmonds, the gifted daughter of the honoured American jurist above mentioned, and one of the most remarkable mediums of this modern movement, united herself with the Catholic Church, her confessor, a Paulist Brother of New York, drove out her obsessing "devils" in due form, after - as he told me - a terrific struggle. Mediumship was anathematized by the late Pope himself, as a dangerous device of the Evil One, and the faithful warned against the familiars of the circle, as his agents for the ruin of souls. There appeared in France, within the past few years, a series of books by the Chevalier des Mousseaux, highly applauded by the Catholic prelates, especially designed to collate the most striking proof of the demoniac agency in the phenomena. They are all valuable repositories of psychic facts one especially, *Les Moeurs et Pratiques des Démons*, which every student of Occultism should read. The industrious author of course convinces no one but Catholics as to his premises, but his facts are most welcome and suggestive. Though there is never a grain of religious orthodoxy in me, and I do not in the least sympathize with the demoniacal theory, yet I find, after learning what I have of Asiatic psychological science, that the Catholics are much nearer right in recognizing and warning against the dangers of mediumship, than the Protestants in blindly denying the reality of the phenomena. Mediumship is a peril indeed, and the last thing I could wish would be to see one whom I was interested in become one. The Hindûs - who have known these phenomena from time immemorial - give the most appropriate name of *bhitta dak,* or demon's post to these unfortunates. I do sincerely hope that sooner or later the experience of India in this matter will be studied, and if mediumship is to be encouraged at all, it shall be under such protective restriction as the ancient Sybils enjoyed in the temple, under the watchful care of initiated priests. This is not the language of a Spiritualist, nor am I one: in the reality of the phenomena and the existence of the psychic force I do most unreservedly believe, but here my concurrence with the Spiritualists ends. For more than twenty years I was of their opinion, and shared, with Mr Owen and Mr Wallace, the conviction that the phenomena could not be attributed to any other agency than that of the departed ones; I could not understand how the intelligence behind the manifestations could be otherwise accounted for, especially that shown in such cases as I have mentioned, where the facts related were unknown to anyone at the séance, and only verified long afterwards in distant countries; but until meeting Madame Blavatsky at the Eddys' I had not even heard of Asiatic Occultism as a science. The tales of travelers and the stories of the Arabian Nights I set down to fanciful exaggeration, and all that was printed about Indian jugglers and the powers of ascetics seemed but accounts of successful prestidigitations. I can now look back to that meeting as the most fortunate event of my life, for it made light shine in all the dark places and sent me out on a mission to help Âryan occult science, which grows more absorbingly interesting with every day. It is my happiness not only to help to enlarge the boundaries of Western science by showing where the secrets of nature and of man may be experimentally studied, and to give Anglo-

Indians a greater respect for the subject nation they rule over, but also to aid in kindling in the bosoms of Indian youths a proper reverence for their glorious ancestry and a desire to imitate them in their noble achievements in Science and Philosophy. This, ladies and gentlemen, is the sole cause of our coming to India; this explains our affectionate relations with the people, our respect for their real Yogis. Each of you looks forward to the day when you will return to your English home; our home is here, and here we mean to end our days.

The handbills announce me as the President of the Theosophical Society, and you gathered here to learn what Theosophy is and what are its relations with Spiritualism.

Let me say then, that in the sense given to it by those who first used it, the word means divine wisdom, or the knowledge of divine wisdom, or the knowledge of divine things. The lexicographers handicap the idea with the suggestion that it means the knowledge of God, the Deity before their minds being a personal one; but such was not the intention of the early Theosophists. Essentially, a Theosophical Society is one which favours man's original acquisition of knowledge about the hidden things of the universe by the education and perfecting of his own latent powers. Theosophy differs as widely from philosophy as it does from theology. It has been truly said that, in investigating the divine nature and attributes, philosophy proceeds entirely by the dialectic method, employing as the basis of its investigation the ideas derived from natural reason; theology, still employing the same method, super adds to the principles of natural reason those derived from authority and revelation. Theosophy, on the contrary, professes to exclude all dialectical process, and to drive all its knowledge of God from direct and immediate intuition and contemplation. This Theosophy dates from the highest antiquity of which we have preserved any records, and every original founder of a religion was a seeker after divine wisdom by the Theosophic process of self-illumination. Where do we find in our day the facilities for pursuing this glorious study? Where are the training schools that are worthy to be called the successors of those of the Neo-Platonists of Alexandria, the Hierophants of Egypt, the Theodidaktoi of Greece, or - and especially - the Rshis of Âryavarta, noblest of all initiates, if we except the stainless, the illuminated Gautama Buddha?

Think for a moment of what this Theosophical study exacts of a man who would really penetrate the mysteries and become a true *illuminatus*. The lusts of the flesh, the pride of life, the prejudices of birth, race, creed (so far as it creates dogmatism) must all be put aside. The body must be made the convenience, instead of the despot of, the higher self. The prison bars of Sense that incarcerate the man of Matter must be unlocked, and while living in and being a factor in the outer world, the Theosophist must be able to look into, enter, act in, and return from, the inner world, fraught with divine truths. Are there - were there ever - such men - such demigods, rather let us say? There were; there *are*. The legends of the past may seem to us tinged with error, wild and fantastic even; but nevertheless such men as these existed and displayed their powers, in many countries, at various epochs.

And nowhere more than in India, this blessed land of the Sun - now so poor, so spiritless, so famished and degraded. This was the home of ancient Theosophy; here - upon these very Himâlayan mountains that tower so high yonder - lived and taught the men who won the prize of divine knowledge, whose wisdom - a fertilizing stream - flowed through Grecian and Egyptian channels towards the West. Believe me or not, as you will, I am fully persuaded that there still linger among these fastnesses, out of the poisoned moral atmosphere of this nineteenth century social life, safe from the blight and persecution of bigotry and intolerant modern superstition, safe from the cruel malice of scepticism - those who are true Theosophists. Neither pessimist nor optimist, I am not satisfied that our race is doomed to destruction, present or future, nor that the moral sense of society can be kept undiminished without constant refreshment from the parent fount. That found I conceive to be Theosophical study and personal illumination, and I regard him as a benefactor to his kind who points out to the sceptical, the despairing, the world-weary, the heart-hungry, that the vanities of the world do not satisfy the soul's aspirations, and true happiness can only be acquired by interior self-development, purification and enlightenment. It is not in accord with the abstract principles of Justice that the world should be left entirely without such exemplars of spiritual wisdom. I do not believe it ever was, or ever will be.

To him who takes up this course of effort the phenomena of mediumship are transcendingly important, for they usher him into the realm of the Unseen, and show him some of the weirdest secrets of our human nature. Along with mediumship he studies vital magnetism, its laws and phenomena, and the Odyle of Baron Richenbach, which together show us the real nature and polarities of this Force, and the fact that it seems to be akin to the one great force that pervades all nature. Further proof he draws from Buchanan's psychometry, and experiments with those whom he finds to be endowed with the psychometrical faculty.

If there are any here to whom this is a new word, I will say that this is a name given by the modern discoverer to a certain power possessed by about one person in four, to receive intuitive impressions of the character of the writer of a letter or the painter of a picture, by direct contact with the manuscript or the painting. Every one of us is constantly leaving the impress of his character upon everything we touch, as the loadstone imparts some of its properties to every needle it is rubbed against. A subtle something - magnetism, or vital fluid, or psychic force - constantly exudes from us. We leave it on the ground and our dog finds us; on our clothing, and the slaver's bloodhound sniffs the scent and tracks the poor runaway to his hiding place. We saturate with it the walls of our houses; and a sensitive psychometrist, upon entering our drawing-room, can unerringly tell, before seeing the family, whether that is a happy home or one of strife. We are surrounded by it as a sensitive vapour, and when we meet each other we silently take in an impression of our mutual congeniality or antipathy. Women have this sense more than men, and many are the instances where a wife's prophetic intuition, unheeded and ridiculed by the husband, in the case of some new acquaintance, has afterwards been recalled with regret that it should have been disregarded. Good psychometrists can even take from any fragment of inanimate matter, such as a bit of an old building, or a shred of an old garment, a vivid impression of all the scenes of its history. In its highest manifestation psychometry becomes true clairvoyance, and when that soul-sight is indeed opened, the eye within us that never grows lustreless shows us the arcana of the Unseen Universe.

Theosophy shows the student that evolution is a fact, but that it has not been partial and incomplete as Darwin's theory makes it. As there has been an evolution in physical nature, the crown and flower of which is physical man, so there has been a parallel evolution in the realm of spirit. The outcome of this is the psychic, or inner man; and just as in this visible nature about us we see myriads of forms lower than ourselves, so the Theosophist finds in the *terra incognita* of the physicist - the realm of the "Unknowable" -countless minor psychical types, with man at the top of the ascending series. Physicists know of the elements only in their chemical or dynamic relations and properties; but he who has mastered the Occult Sciences, finds, dwelling in fire, air, earth, and water, sub-human orders of beings, some inimical, some favourable to man. He not only comes to a knowledge of them, but also to the power of controlling them. The folk-lore of the world has embalmed many truths about this power, which is none the less a fact, although the modern biologist turns up his nose at it. You who come from Ireland or the Scottish Highlands know that these beings exist. I do not surmise this, I *know* it. I speak thus calmly and boldly about the subject, because I have met these proficients of Asiatic Occultism and seen them exercise their power. This is why I ceased to call myself a Spiritualist in 1874, and why, in 1875 I united with others to found a Theosophical Society to promote the study of these natural phenomena. The most wonderful facts of mediumship I have seen produced at will, and in full daylight, by one who had learnt the secret sciences in India and Egypt. Under such circumstances I have seen showers of roses made to fall in a room; letters from people in far countries to drop from space into my lap; heard sweet music, coming from afar upon the air, grow louder and louder until it was in the room, and then die away again out in the still atmosphere until it was no more. I have seen writing made to appear upon paper and slates laid upon the floor, drawings upon the ceiling beyond anyone's reach, pictures upon paper without the employment of pencil or colour, articles duplicated before my very eyes, a living person instantly disappear before my sight, jet black hair cut from a fair-haired person's head, had absent friends and distant scenes shown me in a crystal, and, in America, more than a hundred times, upon opening letters upon various subjects coming to me by the common post from my correspondents in all parts of the world, have found inside, written in their own familiar hand, messages to me from men in India who possess the Theosophical knowledge of natural law. Nay, upon one occasion, I even saw summoned before me as perfectly "materialized" a figure as any that ever stalked out of William Eddy's cabinet of marvels. If it is not strange that the Spiritualist, who sees mediumistic phenomena, but knows nothing of occult science, should believe in the intervention of spirits of the dead, is it any stranger that I, after receiving so many proofs of what the trained human will can accomplish, should be a Theosophist and no longer a Spiritualist? I have not even half exhausted the catalogue of the proofs that have been vouchsafed to me during the last five years as to the reality of Asiatic psychological science, but I hope I have enumerated enough to show you that there are mysteries in India worth seeking, and men *here* who are far more acquainted with nature's occult forces than any of those much credited gentlemen who set themselves up for professors and biologists.

It will be asked what evidence I offer that the intelligent phenomena of the mediums are not to be ascribed to our departed friends. In reply, I ask what unimpeachable evidence is there that they are? If it can be shown that the soul of the living medium can, unconsciously to his physical self, ooze out, and, by its elastic and protean nature, take on the appearance of any deceased person whose image it sees in a visitor's memory; if all the phenomena can be produced at will by an educated psychologist; if, in the æther of science - the *Akâsa* of the Hindûs, the Anima Mundi of the Theosophists, the Astral Light of the Cabalists - the images of all persons and events, and the vibrations of every sound, are eternally preserved - as these occultists affirm and experimentally prove - if all this is true, then why is it necessary to call in the spirits of the dead to explain what may be done by the living? So long as no alternative theory was accessible, the Spiritualists held impregnable ground against materialistic science; theirs was the only possible way to account for what they saw. But, given the alternative, and shown the resources of psychology and the nature of the Unseen Universe, you see the Spiritualists are at once thrown upon the defensive without the ability to silence their critics. The casual observer would say it is impossible, for instance, for that aged Quaker lady's figure to be anything but her own returning soul - that her son could not have been mistaken, and that, if there were any doubt otherwise, her familiar knowledge of their family matters, and even her old habit of alternately plaiting and smoothing out her lawn apron, would identify her amply. But the figure did nothing and said nothing that was not fixed in the son's memory - indelibly stamped there, however long the dormant pictures might have been obscured by fresher images. And the medium's body being entranced and his active vitality transferred to his inner self, or "double," that double could make itself appear under the guise of the dead lady, and catch and comment upon the familiar incidents it found in the son's magnetic atmosphere.

This will be hard for you to comprehend, for our Western scientific discoveries have not yet as yet crossed the threshold of this hidden world of Force. But progress is the law of human thought, and we are now so near the verge of the chasm that divides physical from spiritual science, that it will not be long before we will bridge it. Let this stand as a prophecy; if you bide patiently you will see it fulfilled. This then is the present attitude of parties. The promulgation of our views and of many reports by eye-witnesses of things done by members of the Theosophical Society has been causing great talk all over the world. A large body of the most intelligent Spiritualists have joined us and are giving their countenance to our work. Groups of sympathizers have organized themselves into branches in many different countries. Even here, in Simla, there has sprung up the nucleus of what will be an Anglo-Indian branch. No country in the world affords so wide a field as India for psychological study. What we Europeans call Animal Magnetism has been known here and practiced in its highest perfection for countless centuries. The Hindûs know equally well the life-principle in man, animal and plants. All over India, if search were but made, you would find, in the possession of the natives, many facts that it is most important for Europe and America to know. And you, gentlemen of the civil and military branches of public service, are the proper ones to undertake the work with Hindû help. Be just and kind to them and they will tell you a thousand things they now keep profound secrets among themselves. Our policy is one of general conciliation and cooperation for the discovery of truth. Some tale-bearer has started the report that our Society is preaching a new religion. This is false: the Society has no more a religion of its own than the Royal Asiatic, the Royal Geographical, or the Royal Astronomical. As those societies have their separate sections, each devoted to some to some speciality of research, so have we. We take in persons of all religions and every race, and treat all with equal respect and impartiality. We have royal, noble, and plebeian blood among us. Edison is our member, and Wallace, and Camille Flammarion, and Lord Lindsay, and Baron du Potet, and the octogenarian Cahagnet, and scores of men of that intellectual quality. We have but one passionate and consuming ambition - that of learning what man is, of what nature. Are there any here who sympathize with these aspirations? Any who feel within their hearts the glow of true manhood - one that puts a higher value upon divine wisdom than upon the honours and rewards of the lower life? Come, then, brother dreamers, and let us combine our efforts and our goodwill. Let us see if we cannot win happiness for ourselves in striving to benefit others. Let us do what we can to rescue from the oblivion of centuries that priceless knowledge of divine things which we call THEOSOPHY.

www.ingramcontent.com/pod-product-compliance
Lightning Source LLC
LaVergne TN
LVHW041502070426
835507LV00009B/770